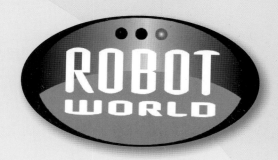

# Robots
# in Dangerous
# Places

## by Steve Parker

amicus

Published by Amicus
P.O. Box 1329
Mankato, MN 56002

Printed in the United States of America, at Corporate
Graphics in North Mankato, Minnesota.

Library of Congress Cataloging-in-Publication Data
Parker, Steve, 1952-
   Robots in dangerous places / by Steve Parker.
      p. cm. – (Robot world)
   Includes index.
   Summary: "Discusses how robots are used to explore
and work in places too dangerous for people. Also
discusses advances in robotics, and how we benefit
from the jobs these robots do"–Provided by publisher.
   ISBN 978-1-60753-072-5 (library binding)
   1. Robotics–Juvenile literature. 2. Robots, Industrial–
Juvenile literature. I. Title.
   TJ211.2.P367 2011
   629.8'92–dc22

                                    2010001124

Created by Appleseed Editions, Ltd.
Designed by Guy Callaby
Edited by Mary-Jane Wilkins
Picture research by Su Alexander

Picture acknowledgements
Title page Volker Steger/Science Photo Library; Contents page Peter
Menzel/Science Photo Library; 4 Mira/Alamy; 5t Hemis/Alamy, b
NASA/Carnegie Mellon University/Science Photo Library; 6 Michael
Rosenfeld/Science Faction/Corbis; 7 Niall Cotton/Alamy; 8 RJH_RF/
Alamy; 9 Hank Morgan/Science Photo Library; 10 Juniors
Bildarchiv/Alamy; 11t Peter Menzel/Science Photo Library, b Gunter
Marx/Alamy; 12 Yanns Arthus-Bertrand/Corbis; 13t Patrick
Landmann/Science Photo Library, b Roger Ressmeyer/Corbis; 14
Peter Menzel/Science Photo Library; 15t Robert Harding Picture
Library/Alamy, b Greenshoots Communications/Alamy; 16 Alexis
Rosenfeld/Science Photo Library; 17 Ralph White/Corbis; 18
Michael Donne/Science Photo Library; 19t Volker Steger/Science
Photo Library, b Philippe Psaila/Science Photo Library; 20t
Ballantine/Alamy, b Philippe Psaila/Science Photo Library; 21 Mike
Blake/Reuters/Corbis; 22 Philippe Psaila/Science Photo Library; 23t
Hawker Siddeley Dynamics/Science Photo Library, b US Air Force/
Science Photo Library; 24 US Navy photo by Mass Communication
Specialist Seaman Apprentice Joshua Adam Nuzzo; 25t Andrew
Fox/Alamy, b Richard Wareham Fotografie/Alamy; 26 Louise
Murray/Science Photo Library; 27t ni press photos/Alamy, b
Francoise Demulder/Corbis; 28 Brian Snyder/Corbis; 29t Rex
Features, b Omni wheel assortment courtesy of AndyMark,Inc.
Front cover Yiorgos Karahalis/Reuters/Corbis

DAD0040
32010

9 8 7 6 5 4 3 2 1

# Contents

# Beware—Danger!

**W**anted: workers for **hazardous** tasks. Must be able to detect deadly fumes from volcanoes, check underground drains, measure invisible **radioactive** rays, and dive to the seabed to examine undersea pipelines. Must be fearless, reliable, obedient, and hardworking. No holidays, no pay, no free time. Apply today!

## Hazards Everywhere

Robots are ideal workers for dangerous places. They can be made much tougher than people, with extra-strong outer casings that resist heat, cold, and chemicals. They are not affected by deadly fumes or radiation. They don't need air to breathe, food to eat, or water to drink. They can be fitted with special equipment for their tasks, such as cameras to see in the dark, powerful grippers to hold tightly, and sharp blades to cut.

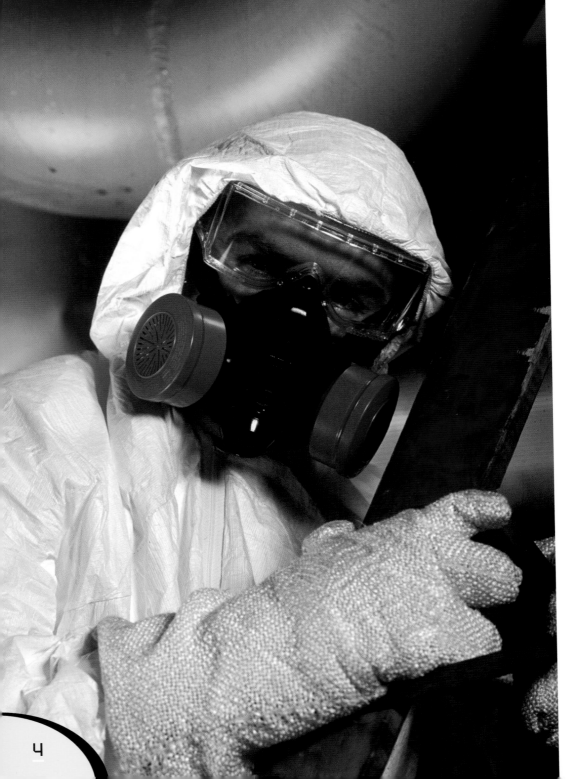

◀◀ *Where there are harmful substances, chemicals, or rays, people must wear specially made protective suits. Robots do not need this kind of protection.*

## Just a Machine

All around the world, robots carry out thousands of hazardous tasks daily. They check for bombs, explosive mines, and go into buildings that might collapse. They fight fires and carry out secret military missions, such as spying on an enemy. Unlike people, they cannot be frightened or confused. They remain cool in the face of danger.

Some of these risk-taking robots are very clever, with a powerful computer "brain," great strength, and other amazing abilities. But they are not living beings. One great advantage of using robots is that if there's an accident, human lives are not at risk. Robots are merely machines.

 *Erupting volcanoes are no places for humans, but robots can withstand extreme heat, so they can collect samples of rocks and gases, as well as study the chemicals from which they are made.*

## ROBOT SUPERSTAR

### Dante Explores

*During the 1990s, the Dante series of robots crawled into Antarctic volcanoes to find out what was in volcanic gases and fumes. Dante 2 was more than 9 feet (3 m) tall, with a spider-like shape and long legs. Wires connected it to the control base a safe distance away. Dante edged over the volcano's steep rim, ready to clamber down into the crater, filled with choking fumes and hotter than an oven. Then the connecting wire broke, and Dante and the scientists had to give up.*

# Rough and Tough

Every part of a risk-taking robot is designed to cope with many hazards as well as extreme conditions. These include intense cold, great heat, falling objects, poisonous fumes, and splashes of dangerous chemicals. This is why most robots designed for dangerous places have strong, wrap-around outer cases made of metal or other very tough materials.

### Hot and Cold

Robots are designed to cope with specific types of danger. When a person touches an object that is hotter than about 104°F (40°C), it feels uncomfortably hot. A few degrees more and human skin starts to feel pain and suffer burns. Robots can touch objects that are many times hotter—provided their engineers make them from suitable materials.

*Cryogenic storage means keeping items at incredibly low temperatures. If we touched any of them, our skin and flesh would freeze solid in an instant, so robots often take over.*

Hot-bots are made of **thermoresistant** materials, which means they can withstand temperatures of several hundred degrees. These materials include certain metals, special plastics, and combined or composite materials such as glass-reinforced plastic (fiberglass plastic) and carbon-fiber composite.

### The Importance of Materials

If a robot is likely to get very hot only for a short time, then only its outer covering needs to be thermoresistant. But if it's going to be very hot for a long time, then the robot's working parts inside, such as its motors, levers, and gears, also need to be able to resist heat. This gives robot engineers and materials scientists many new challenges.

Robots in very cold places are made from **cryoresistant** materials. Some of them have small electric heaters inside, powered by their batteries, to keep their inner parts warm.

*Human eyes would be permanently damaged by the intense light of this flame. A welding robot has no such problem and is not affected by the flame's heat either.*

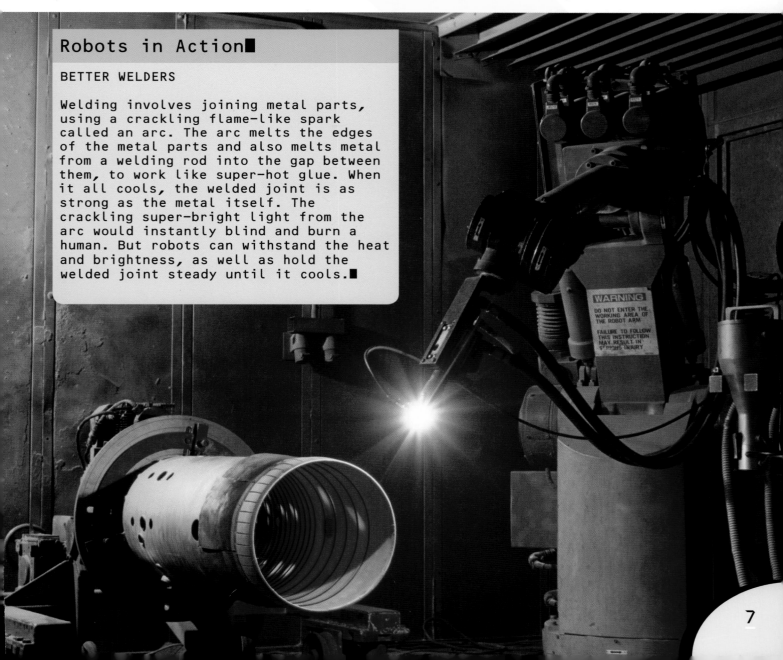

## Robots in Action■

### BETTER WELDERS

Welding involves joining metal parts, using a crackling flame-like spark called an arc. The arc melts the edges of the metal parts and also melts metal from a welding rod into the gap between them, to work like super-hot glue. When it all cools, the welded joint is as strong as the metal itself. The crackling super-bright light from the arc would instantly blind and burn a human. But robots can withstand the heat and brightness, as well as hold the welded joint steady until it cools.■

WARNING
DO NOT ENTER THE
WORKING AREA OF
THE ROBOT ARM

FAILURE TO FOLLOW
THIS INSTRUCTION
MAY RESULT IN
SERIOUS INJURY

# Under Control

A typical robot carries out some jobs and tasks by itself. It has moving parts, such as motors, wheels, levers, and gears. Robots detect what is going on around them, using cameras as eyes, microphones as ears, and contact **sensors** as skin. Instructions, orders, or programs come from their masters —humans. Then they carry out their tasks in an automatic way, but some robots are more automatic than others.

### Simple Tasks

Simple robots are partly controlled by people. They do a job, for example, drilling into polar ice to see how thick it is. This is part of scientific research looking into **global warming** and **climate change**. The robot drillers send their results to their human controllers. Then they wait for the next instruction about where to move and drill next.

*Global warming is a huge problem. Robots can help us study how fast it happens by measuring the temperature of the polar ocean and the ice thickness.*

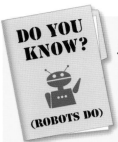

### DO YOU KNOW?

(ROBOTS DO)

### SnoMotes

SnoMotes are groups or swarms of small, mobile robots that travel across ice and snow to collect information about global warming. They are similar to mini-snowmobiles, and they carry cameras and record temperature, ice hardness, snow depth, and other measurements. Members of each swarm communicate with each other, and they determine among themselves what to do next. They face daily risks such as deep **crevasses** (cracks), **avalanches**, and falling through melting ice.

### Clever Robots

Very clever robots need almost no orders from people. These robots are called **autonomous**. This means that they can make decisions and control themselves for long periods of time. They have powerful computer brains. If they go to a dangerous place, they decide how to get there, what to do, and when to escape.

### Wired and Wireless

Some robots are joined to a central control or base by a long cable or wire, called a tether. Orders or instructions are sent as electrical signals along the wire, telling the robot what to do. Other robots are wireless—they receive and send information by radio signals. This means they are free to move around, so long as they stay within range of the radio waves. One problem with this way of communicating is that radio waves cannot travel very far through water. So underwater robots usually need tethers.

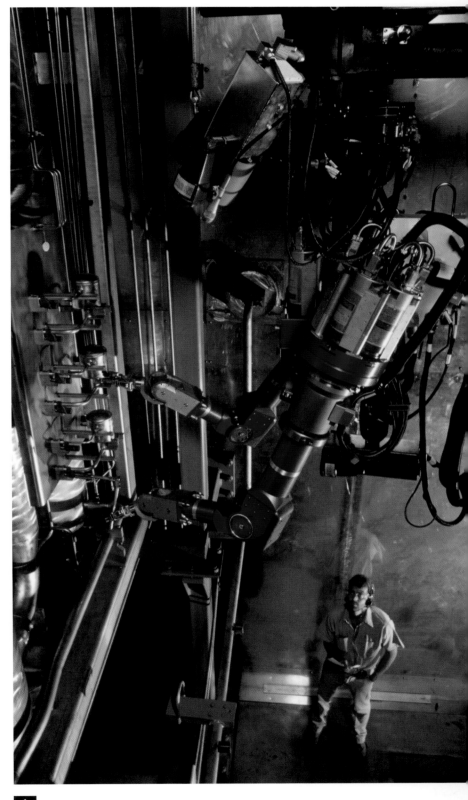

Many mobile robots have cables to bring electricity and also high-pressure oil or gas pipes to power their movements. These cables, pipes, and tethers must bend and straighten perhaps millions of times without a leak or crack, and they limit where the robots can go.

# Disaster Scenes

Many natural disasters happen around the world: earthquakes, landslides, mudslides, **tsunamis**, cave collapses, and volcanic eruptions. All of them can damage buildings, especially large buildings such as skyscrapers, schools, offices, and factories. It's dangerous for human rescuers to go into damaged, weak buildings, which might cave in at any moment or catch fire and fill with choking fumes. Often robots undertake rescue missions instead.

## Search and Rescue

Search-and-rescue robots, or SARbots, are usually quite small so they can crawl through narrow spaces in broken buildings. They have powerful electric motors and rubber caterpillar tracks to give them a strong grip, as they climb over rubble or up and down stairs. They also have lights to shine in the darkness, cameras to see, and sensitive microphones to hear people calling for help. Other types of sensors include **infrared** cameras to detect the heat given off by the bodies of trapped people.

▼ *Disaster rescue teams include people, dogs to sniff and hear, equipment such as sensitive microphones to listen, and robots to explore inside broken buildings.*

## Careful Control

SARbots are usually attached to their control center by long cables or tethers that trail behind them as they explore in a disaster zone. Their instructions travel along the cable, as well as electricity for their motors, so the robots do not need heavy batteries. Pictures and other information from the robots' sensors go back along the cable to the control center. Here the people controlling the robot usually have someone who knows the layout of the building or site, who can guide the robot.

▶▶ *The Blue Dragon explorer robot snakes its way through jumbles of rubble and small gaps, gripping with its caterpillar tracks as it searches for survivors.*

## ROBO-FUTURE

### Robot Paramedic

*New search-and-rescue robots may be able to carry food, water, and medicines, such as pain-killing drugs. The SARbot would move close to a trapped person and pass over the supplies as needed. The people at the control base can see and hear what's happening and talk to the trapped person, using a speaker on the rescue robot.*

▼ *If human cavers cannot fit through a narrow gap, they can send in a slim robot to take a first look at the next cavern.*

# Unseen Killers

**N**uclear power plants make about one-twelfth of all the electricity that people use around the world. The safety and security of these power plants are especially important. Nuclear accidents are rare, but when they occur, they can be massive disasters. Even when a power plant is running perfectly, there are areas inside where people cannot go. Enter the robots!

### Dangerous Rays
Nuclear power plant fuel is a form of the **heavy metal uranium**. It is radioactive, which means that it gives off invisible rays and particles known as radiation. These can harm people and all living things, so it's vital to contain and control radioactivity. If any leaks or escapes, it could spread far and wide. Even on normal days, workers in a nuclear power station must be aware of radioactivity levels and keep out of high-risk areas.

▼ *In 1986, the nuclear power plant at Chernobyl in the Ukraine blew up. This caused immense damage and people had to leave nearby towns such as Pripyat. Robots still help clear the deadly radioactive material.*

⬆ Robot arms move radioactive liquids safely in a nuclear research center. If countries generate more nuclear power in the future, these types of robots will become more important.

### How Robots Are Used

Nuclear power plants have a variety of robot-like machines such as grippers, arms, and **manipulators**, which work in areas with high radioactivity. The metals, plastics, and other materials in the robots are not affected by the rays and particles. Some of these robots are mobile and automatic. Others are controlled by people who can see what they are doing through a glass screen that protects against radioactivity.

### Toxic Gases

More unseen dangers include poisonous or **toxic** gases, such as deadly **carbon monoxide** from some forms of burning and choking **ammonia** or **chlorine** gases from chemicals. If a factory accident leaks these gases, people must leave at once. Then a robot may be sent in to find the problem and check the level of gas with its specially designed "nose" or sniffer sensors.

## ROBOT SUPERSTAR

### HERO

The HERO robots were designed in the 1980s to teach people about robots and how they work, as well as to be entertaining and fun. You could buy the robots ready-made or as a kit, so that you learned about the inside parts as you fitted them together. Different HERO models can sense their surroundings, move around, avoid obstacles, and even talk, using simple words and phrases. HERO 2000 has been programmed to pick up and deal with cans that might contain leaking radioactive material.

HERO 1

# In the Dark

Mines, tunnels, and pipelines are dangerous places. Not only are they dark, they may also be full of gas, poisonous fumes, oil, chemicals, and other substances. Cleaning and checking inside them is very risky for people. That's why many kinds of robots venture into the blackness.

Kurt the inspection robot checks sewers for leaks and problems. It has its own power supply and guidance system to come out of the pipe network at the correct place.

### Pipeline Pigs

Big chemical factories, **oil refineries**, and industrial centers may have many miles (km) of pipes and tubes to check, clean, and repair. Wider, longer pipelines snake for thousands of miles (km) across the land, carrying oil, gas, water, and other materials. Robot machines called pipeline inspection gauges or PIGs—known as pipeline pigs—travel inside the pipes. The PIGs clean inside the pipes, remove blockages, and detect breaks or leaks.

### Smarter PIGs

Pipeline pigs become more useful and autonomous every year. The Explorer II PIG is one of the latest to inspect gas and oil pipelines. This PIG moves along under its own power, instead of being pushed along by the movement of the material in the pipe. It can slow down or speed up and sends out combined **electromagnetic waves**, which are altered by the pipe around them. The PIG detects any cracks, breaks, rust, or other problems in the pipe as changed patterns in the waves.

### Around the Bend

Explorer II's computer brain, powerful battery packs, **drive units**, sensors, and other parts are enclosed in 11 linked units, which are about 8 feet (2.4 m) long. This design allows it to curve around bends in the pipe like a giant string of sausages.

The Trans-Alaska Oil Pipeline is 802 miles (1,290 km) long and has pipes 48 inches (122 cm) wide. Several kinds of robots regularly pass through, including scraper PIGs, kink-sensing PIGs, and rust-detecting PIGs.

People stay well away from a mine blast, but robots near the explosion monitor that all is well and warn of a possible collapse.

## ROBO-FUTURE

### Robot Miners

Mines and quarries are hazardous places. Miners are at risk from rockfalls, roof collapses, poisonous gases, choking dust, and explosive accidents. Robots are taking over more mining tasks. Massive robot dumper trucks trundle on programmed routes around sites. Robot roof fixers fit panels after a tunnel is blasted or drilled, to make it safe for workers. If an area fills up with dust or sand, a robot "mole" can burrow down to see what has happened.

# Deep Water

A summer paddle at the seaside is great fun. But out in the ocean, there are hazards of all kinds—huge waves, strong winds, powerful tides, and surging currents. Under the surface of the sea are the black depths, with intense cold and immense pressure.

### Underwater Rovers

For many years, robots have dived deep under water. Their tasks vary from checking a ship for cracks, to observing ocean wildlife, exploring the seabed for valuable minerals, and finding treasure in sunken shipwrecks.

Some underwater robots are operated by remote control from a ship on the surface. Others are more autonomous and able to work on their own. Most are known as **ROVs**—remotely operated underwater vehicles. Radio signals cannot travel through water, so ROVs have long cables or wires, known as tethers, to supply their electricity and carry information down and up.

The smartest ROVs are far more than simple remote-controlled devices. For example, they can sense sudden water currents that might tilt them over and alter their propellers, rudders, and fins so they stay upright and steady, all without human help.

*A diver in a deep-sea pressure suit checks the ROV Achilles, which does not need any kind of suit. The Achilles series of deep-water robots can descend below 3,281 feet (1,000 m).*

## Corals and Canyons

ROVs carry out many tasks, especially surveys of ocean life and the seabed. Scientists guide them through coral reefs, into underwater canyons, and along the bottom. They watch the scene on the ROV's cameras as it records water temperature, pressure, currents, and other measurements. This information helps us understand how underwater earthquakes cause massive tsunami waves and how global warming is affecting the oceans.

### Argo

In 1985, the wreck of the giant passenger ship Titanic, which sank in 1912, was found about 12,467 feet (3,800 m) below the surface on the bed of the North Atlantic Ocean. Here the water's enormous pressure would kill a person instantly. The wreck was found by cameras on the sledge-like device Argo, towed just above the ocean floor by a massively long cable from a ship above. Was Argo a robot? Probably not. It could only take pictures and echo soundings or sonar measurements. It could not move or make decisions on its own.

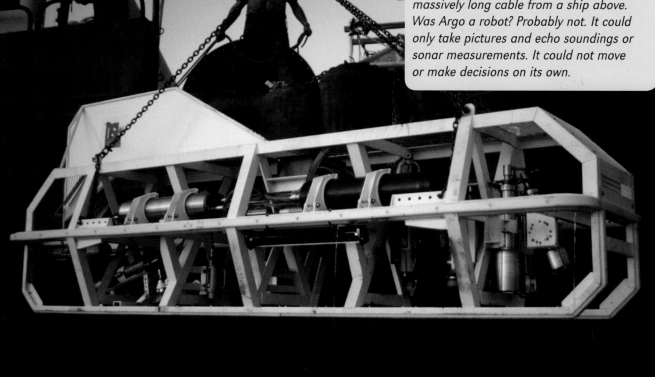

*Crew members prepare to lower Argo into the sea, on its way to detecting the wreck of the* Titanic.

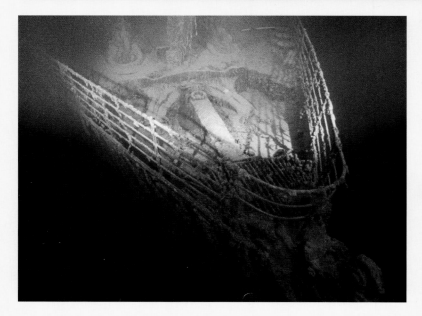

*After the* Titanic *was found on the seabed, several ROVs and manned craft, such as Alvin, studied how it had sunk and what was left.*

# Fight that Fire!

Human firefighters brave perilous conditions, such as blazing flames, burning heat, choking smoke, deadly fumes, collapsed buildings, and the risk of explosion. More and more robots are helping explore fire scenes, checking for hazards, and making an area safe.

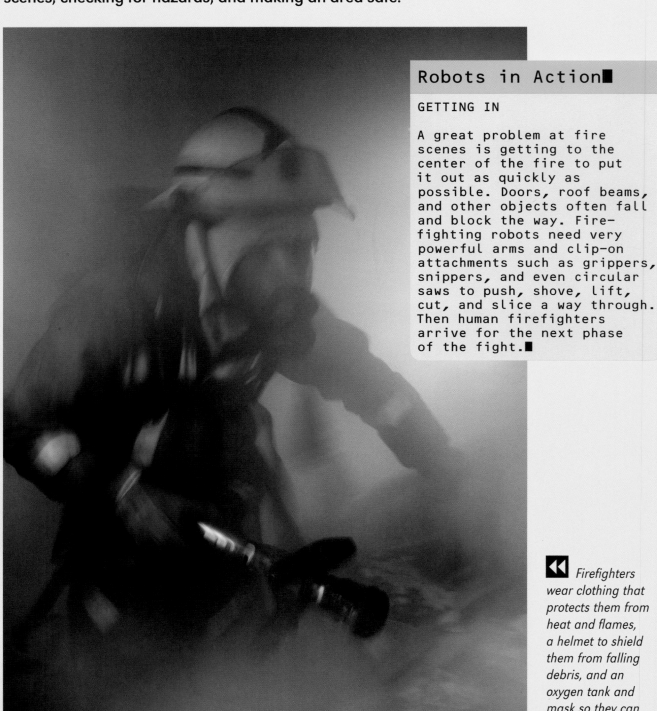

## Robots in Action■

GETTING IN

A great problem at fire scenes is getting to the center of the fire to put it out as quickly as possible. Doors, roof beams, and other objects often fall and block the way. Fire-fighting robots need very powerful arms and clip-on attachments such as grippers, snippers, and even circular saws to push, shove, lift, cut, and slice a way through. Then human firefighters arrive for the next phase of the fight.■

◀◀ *Firefighters wear clothing that protects them from heat and flames, a helmet to shield them from falling debris, and an oxygen tank and mask so they can breathe. Robots do not risk their lives —they are not alive.*

### First at the Scene

Firefighting robots come in various shapes and sizes, depending on the jobs they do. They are strong, tough, and heat resistant, especially to flames and falling items. Scout robots search and explore, usually on a long electrical cable or tether. Like SARbots, they are small and slim so they can fit through narrow gaps. Many have tracks or are multi-wheeled, so they can climb stairs and trundle over rubble. Their cameras take pictures of the scene and send them back to display screens at the control base. They also have temperature sensors, and some carry chemical sensors to detect dangerous fumes and gases.

### Damping Down

Bigger, stronger robots carry a water hose or foam sprayer to the best position for aiming at the fire. The hose trails along behind. Water and foam hoses are heavy to pull and when they are turned on, they give a strong jerk, so they need to be held very firmly. Cameras on these robots allow their human controllers to see where to spray. Gradually the robots put out the flames and damp down very hot objects, such as glowing metal and smoldering wood.

▶▶ *This red fire extinguisher can be aimed and squirted by its robot, which moves close to the flames on heatproof caterpillar tracks.*

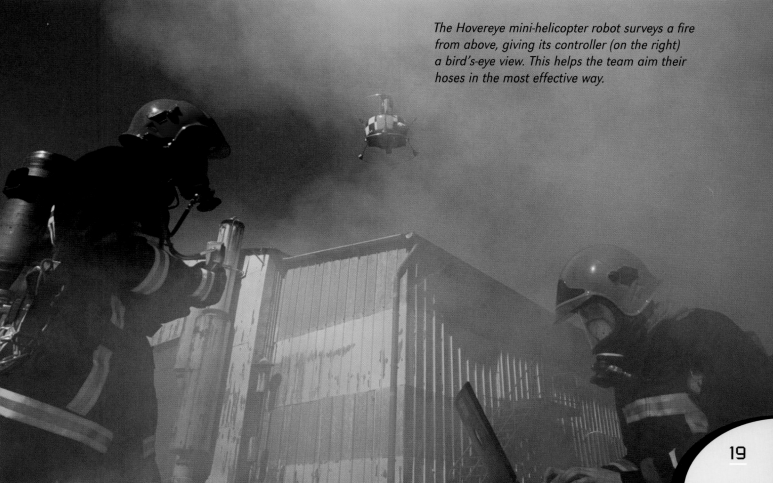

*The Hovereye mini-helicopter robot surveys a fire from above, giving its controller (on the right) a bird's-eye view. This helps the team aim their hoses in the most effective way.*

# Robots at War

Few places are more dangerous than a war zone or battlefield. Army soldiers, air force pilots, and navy sailors risk serious injury and death. Military robots are used for many different tasks to save lives and prevent suffering.

### On the Battlefield

Armies fight with tanks, armored cars, missile-launching trucks, and soldiers on foot. Robot versions of all these are being tested to see whether they can prevent soldiers from dying or suffering serious injuries.

▼ Big tanks are driven by people. Mini-tanks are well-protected robot versions that go ahead of troops to send back information about enemy forces.

▶▶ This fighting robot has a gun mounting on top that can fire a variety of clip-on weapons, including bullets, rocket-propelled grenades, and high-pressure gas jets.

Human pilots guide the Team Terrahawk robot vehicle on a test run before the DARPA Grand Challenge.

Every few years, the U.S. Defense Advanced Research Projects Agency (DARPA) holds its Grand Challenge in a remote area. Unmanned robotic vehicles have to find their way around a complicated route and carry out a series of tasks by themselves, with no human control. The Grand Challenge is fun, but it also helps advance robot technology. It also shows how, one day, supplies might be carried around a war zone by robot trucks.

Could robot soldiers replace human ones? Any robot can suddenly go bad. A rogue robot with a machine gun or grenade launcher might be as likely to fire at its own side as at the enemy.

### Against the Law

Designing robots to attack and kill people goes against the three laws of robotics. These are not real laws but imaginary rules made up by science-fiction writer Isaac Asimov in 1942. The first law says that a robot should not injure a human being or allow a human being to come to harm. Military chiefs would probably say that the laws are designed for peacetime. In wartime, anything goes—even killer-bots.

## ROBO-FUTURE

### Starship Troopers

*The three* Starship Troopers *movies (1997, 2004, 2008) feature massive battles between humans and aliens, including spider-like Bugs. Parts of the story were based on a 1959 book of the same name by Robert Heinlein. In the book, the soldiers wear powered-armor suits, which copy their movements and make them much bigger, stronger, and more dangerous. Also in this future time, medical advances heal the human troopers' wounds very quickly— almost like fitting a new part to a robot.*

# Eye in the Sky

In future wars, there may be many kinds of military robots on the battlefield—and above it, too. One of the best ways to spy on an enemy is from the sky. Already there are many types of robot aircraft called **drones**, which fly over enemy regions or areas where there are suspicious activities. Their job is to sneak in, spy by taking photographs, and escape as quickly as possible.

### Under the Radar

Drones are known as unmanned aerial vehicles or UAVs—they have no pilots or crew. Usually they fly very low, where they cannot be detected by the other side's **radar**. They take photographs and send these back to base in the form of radio signals. The photographs show information such as the number of tanks at an army base or aircraft at an air base.

### Jamming Signals

Some drones are mainly remote controlled by radio signals from their base. Their human masters tell them where to fly and when to take pictures. But the enemy may detect the control signals to the drone or the photograph signals it sends back. The enemy could then block or jam these radio signals, or send more powerful signals to take over the drone, and make it crash or fly to their own base.

▼ *The CPX4 drone is a quadrocopter, with four separate whirling rotors to hover and move through the air. It can stay up for 30 minutes and take hundreds of pictures with its central camera.*

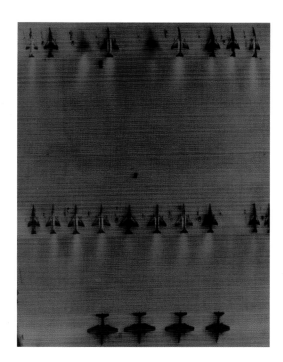

◀◀ *Infrared or heat-sensitive images, such as this picture of an air base, can be taken at night, when it's very difficult to detect the quiet drone in the darkness.*

### Radio Silence

Clever drones need fewer instructions. Their computers, **satnavs**, and **GPS** equipment have enough information to decide where to go and what to photograph. The information is stored onboard until the drone returns to base, so the drone can complete its mission without receiving or sending radio signals —known as radio silence. The silence makes it more difficult for the enemy to detect, as does the drone's small size and quietness.

▼ *The 27-foot (8.22 m) long Predator spyplane is armed with a Hellfire missile under its right wing. The ball-shaped camera under the nose swivels around to point at any angle.*

### ROBOT SUPERSTAR

### Warrior and Predator

*The MQ-1C Sky Warrior first flew in 2008. It will replace the MQ-1 Predator, which has spied on many regions. Warrior is 26 feet (8 m) long, with wings that measure 56 feet (17 m) across. That's big enough to carry a pilot, but Warrior doesn't need one. It flies at almost 155 miles per hour (250 km/h) and can take thousands of photographs—and even shoot Hellfire or Stinger missiles.*

# Robo Navy

Robotic ships and submarines carry out many military tasks. One is **reconnaissance**—patrolling an area to look, listen, and sense anything strange or unusual. Like reconnaissance aircraft, these unmanned ships find their way using satellite navigation. Some of them have guns or even torpedoes (underwater missiles) so they can fire back if attacked.

### Robo-patrols

The robot reconnaissance boat Spartan Scout was designed for the U.S. Navy. Dozens are now used by other countries, too, for various purposes. Spartan Scout can patrol a harbor or coastline to look for smugglers trying to bring cargo into a country illegally, to check for fishing boats in places where fish are protected, and to find terrorists who might be planning an attack.

AMN 1, standing for Autonomous Maritime Navigation, is a U.S. Navy test craft. Here it speeds through its trial runs, controlling itself, although a boat pilot and an engineer take a ride, just in case things go wrong.

### Dangers at Sea

Spartan Scout is almost 23 feet (7 m) long and weighs 2.2 tons (2 t). It records what happens using daylight and night-time cameras, a microphone, **radar**, and other sensors. It detects other boats, explosive mines, submarines, and other dangers. After being programmed by its human masters, this robo-boat can work on its own using satnav for up to 48 hours, or it can be operated by remote control from a ship.

### Ahoy There!

If Spartan Scout finds a suspicious boat, the controllers can watch the scene through its cameras. They can also speak to the boat's crew using a loudspeaker on Spartan Scout and hear what the crew says through its microphones. If someone shoots, the robot boat can fire back, using its powerful machine gun.

▲ *Ordinary satellite navigation, as used in cars, is not as accurate as the military version, which has special radio code signals to pinpoint a location within 3.3 to 6.5 feet (1 to 2 m).*

▼ *Big waves and jagged rocks are serious dangers, but a shipwrecked robot is far better than putting human life in peril on the sea.*

## Robots in Action■

### SPY IN THE WATER

Robotic spy boats are programmed to move slowly and quietly through the water, usually under cover of night, into a forbidden area. They take photographs of boats, ships, buildings, and other objects on the shore, and then sneak back to their mother ship out at sea. These boats have infrared cameras, GPS systems, radar, and also sonar, which uses sound waves to bounce off nearby objects and identify their location and distance.■

# Bomb Disposal

Few things are as dangerous as an unexploded bomb. Old wartime bombs, modern terrorist bombs, forgotten land mines, and improvised explosive devices or **IEDs** cause tragedies daily around the world. For many years, robots have helped prevent these disasters and save people from horrific injuries and even death.

*Bomb-disposal robot Remotec HD-1 prepares to pick up a dangerous object. It has a color camera so its operator can see the scene, all-terrain caterpillar tracks, and a telescopic arm with a grabbing pincer.*

## Mechanical Fingers

Bomb disposal experts are trained to examine an explosive device, disarm or **defuse** it so it cannot go off, take it apart carefully, and get rid of the materials safely. Where possible, they send a robot to approach the device. It has various cameras and microphones as well as manipulator arms fitted with grippers, cutters, and similar tools. With the help of its operator, the robot disposer stays calm and cool under pressure.

## Tricks and Traps

Using a robot, bomb disposal experts can study a device, hear noises such as a ticking timer, and poke or move parts, all from a safe distance. Bomb makers often build tricks and traps into their devices, such as vibration sensors that can feel a trembling hand or that make the bomb explode if it is moved. So bomb robots must be precise, accurate, and engineered to very high standards, in case a slight jolt sets off a vibration sensor.

▼ *In this real-life scene, an army bomb disposal robot moves cautiously towards a possible terrorist device—to find out that it's a trick or hoax and the "bomb" is false.*

Some bomb disposal robots can open a car door, look inside, check a suspect device, lift it out carefully, and carry it away to a safer place, ready to be exploded. Despite the combined skills of an expert human operator and a robot, accidents do happen. Some robots are blown to pieces. But that's a tiny price to pay for saving a human life.

◀◀ *In another real-life scene, a bomb has just exploded in a car. In this case, the bomb-detecting robot was also damaged but eventually repaired.*

# War and Peace

Around the world, people continue to face hazards, such as natural disasters, accidents, and wars. Designers and engineers are building improved robots that are stronger, smarter, and more skilled. These can prevent more people being injured or killed in the future.

Various versions of the PackBot series of robots are specialized to "sniff" the air for traces of explosives, detect different rays and waves, listen for suspicious noises, or carry out a suicide mission by setting off a bomb.

## Smart Wheels

Robots sometimes find themselves in small places where it is difficult to move around. One answer is to fit them with special wheels. These are ball shaped and have several small rollers or discs spread around the surface. By varying the speed and direction of the entire wheel and its rollers or discs, the robot can move forward, backward, sideways, and even spin around on the spot. Bomb disposal robots have these wheels, as well as robots that undertake more light-hearted activities, such as playing sports and dancing.

### Robots on the Road

*Robot Wars* was a competition in the U.S. that became a TV series in the UK. For the shows, robots, their equipment, and their human operators turned up at a sports center, stadium, or similar venue. People came to these live events to watch the action, support their favorites, and cheer the winners. It was not only fun but also useful. It helped inventors and engineers come up with new ideas that could be applied to robots with real work to do in factories or in dirty or dangerous situations.

 *Robot Wars pitted various kinds of fun-fighting robots against each other and also encouraged progress in robot design and technology.*

## ROBO-FUTURE

### Octobot

*Like a combination of octopus and crab, Octobot is a test version, or prototype, of a new kind of undersea robot. It is designed to go into deep, dark water, move around using its four claw-like grabbers, and find its way by touch alone. Its outer surface is covered with tiny strip-shaped touch sensors, called electronic strain gauges, each about half as wide as a human hair. The robot can detect the slightest touch as it feels its way along and even react to water currents. Future versions may help repair oil rigs and undersea pipelines or take samples of rocks and mud from the ocean floor.*

*Rollers called omni wheels make robots much more maneuverable or agile and able to get out of tight spots.*

# Glossary

**ammonia**
A dangerous chemical. As a gas, ammonia can damage the human body or even kill people by harming the lungs.

**arc**
A continuous hot, bright spark produced by a very powerful electric current.

**autonomous**
A machine or device that mostly controls itself and works on its own, without human control, as most robots do.

**avalanche**
A sliding mass of snow and ice that rolls or tumbles down a slope with unstoppable force.

**carbon monoxide**
A dangerous gas, usually produced by burning fuel. Carbon monoxide can damage the human body and even kill people by suffocation (being unable to breathe).

**chlorine**
A dangerous chemical. As a gas, chlorine can damage the human body or even kill people by harming the lungs and airways.

**climate change**
Changes in day-to-day weather and long-term climate, mainly because of global warming. This is caused by increasing amounts of some gases in the Earth's atmosphere, for example, carbon dioxide produced by burning fossil fuels and other fuels.

**crevasse**
A deep slit or crack in snow or ice.

**cryoresistant material**
A substance that is not damaged by extremely low temperatures, for example, below −148°F (−100°C).

**defuse**
To make safe a bomb or similar device, so it cannot explode.

**drive units**
Devices that make a robot or similar machine move along. These are usually electric motors.

**drone**
The general name for an unmanned vehicle or robot, especially a flying one. They mainly control themselves or can be operated by humans by remote control.

**electromagnetic waves**
Waves of combined electrical and magnetic energy, including radio waves, microwaves, light rays, and X-rays.

**global warming**
The gradual heating up of the Earth as a result of increasing amounts of some gases in the atmosphere, especially the carbon dioxide produced when we burn fossil fuels and other fuels.

**GPS**
Stands for Global Positioning System—more than 20 satellites that travel around the Earth and send out radio signals. These are detected by a GPS receiver to show the receiver's position and help find the way or navigate. Often called satnav.

**hazardous**
Possibly dangerous or harmful.

**heavy metal**
A metal which is very heavy or weighty, such as lead or uranium.

**IED**
Stands for improvized explosive device. This is a bomb made from easily available materials, which have been adapted, rather than being purpose built.

**infrared**
Light with waves slightly longer than red light waves, that our eyes cannot see, but which some animals' eyes can. Infrared rays carry heat.

**manipulators**
Devices that handle or hold something carefully and move it or its parts precisely.

**oil refineries**
Huge industrial areas where crude oil, or petroleum, is turned into hundreds of useful products, from gasoline and other fuels to paints and varnishes.

### radar
Sending out radio signals and detecting them when they bounce off an object. This shows the size, shape, and distance from the object.

### radioactive
Sending out harmful but invisible rays and tiny particles called radiation, that can damage living things, including the human body.

### reconnaissance
Looking around an area, perhaps in secret, to gather information.

### ROV
Stands for remotely operated vehicle. ROVs are usually underwater craft controlled by a person, or craft that are robotic and mainly able to control themselves.

### satnav
Short for satellite navigation, which is finding the way using a GPS receiver that detects radio signals from satellites going around the Earth.

### sensors
Devices that detect and measure something, such as a camera that measures light, a microphone that measures sound, or a magnetometer that measures magnetic forces.

### thermoresistant material
A substance that is not damaged by extremely high temperatures, for example, above 212°F (100°C), (the boiling temperature of water).

### toxic
Poisonous or harmful in some way, often describing dangerous chemicals.

### tsunami
A huge wave or series of waves set off by an undersea earthquake or volcanic eruption. The wave crashes onto the shore and causes immense damage.

### uranium
A type of metal that is very hard and heavy. Some forms are radioactive.

### welding rod
A long stick-like metal rod used to weld or join metal parts. The welding rod is heated and melts into the narrow gap between the metal parts.

# Further Reading

**Gifford, Clive.** *Robots.* New York: Atheneum, 2008.

**Piccock, Charles.** *Future Tech: From Personal Robots to Motorized Monocycles.* Washington, D.C.: National Geographic, 2009.

**Hyland, Tony.** *High-risk Robots.* North Mankato: Smart Apple Media, 2008.

**Ferrari, Mario.** *Building Robots with LEGO Mindstorms NXT.* Rockland: Syngress, 2007.

# Web Sites

### Robot World News
Robot World News covers the top news stories on robotics, artificial intelligence, and related areas, plus fun information on robots such as toys.
**www.robotworldnews.com**

### Robot Video Clips
Watch video clips of all kinds of robots in action.
**www.pbs.org/wgbh/nova/robots/clips**

### Remotely Operated Vehicles (ROV)
Remotely Operated Vehicles (ROV) covers unoccupied, highly maneuverable underwater robots operated by a person aboard a surface vessel.
**http://oceanexplorer.noaa.gov/technology/subs/rov/rov.html**

# Index

CC

**Central Childrens**

NOV    2010